THE GREEK GODS AND HEROES

Ancient Greece for Kids

Children's Ancient History

The Greek myths are full of exciting adventures of gods and mortal heroes. Who were they? What did they do? Read on and find out!

THE GREEK GODS

In Greek mythology, the first rulers of everything were the Titans, under their leader Cronos. Cronos' children, led by Zeus, Poseidon, and Hades, rose up and defeated the Titans and became the rulers of the universe.

In the myths, the gods are powerful, but sometimes foolish. They get angry and upset; they fall in love; and they hold grudges, often for years. They act, in some ways, like self-interested high-school students with super powers.

Here are some of the greatest and most powerful gods and goddesses:

ZEUS

ZEUS

Zeus became ruler of the universe after the Olympian gods defeated the Titans. (They are called Olympians because Greeks thought the home of the gods was on Mount Olympus.) Zeus was also the ruler of the skies and the weather, and his main weapon was thunderbolts which he could throw at lands, cities, or people that angered him.

Zeus was married to Hera, but he carried on affairs with many Titans, gods, and humans. He is the father of many of the other gods.

POSEIDON

After Zeus and his brothers defeated the Titans, they let chance decide who got to be ruler of each part of the world. Poseidon became the ruler of the oceans. Under him he had gods and demi-gods like Triton and Nereid. Sailors and travelers made offerings to Poseidon in hopes of safe journeys.

POSEIDON

Poseidon also had the power of creating storms, tidal waves, and earthquakes—the Greeks said that the sound of an earthquake was the horses of Poseidon running under the ground.

HADES

Hades ruled the underworld, where people went after they died. He does not take part in many of the myths, except those in which one of the heroes visits the underworld to speak to an ancestor or rescue someone. Hades tricked Persephone, whom he loved, and forced her to live with him for three months out of the year.

HADES

HAEDES AND PERSEPHONE

Persephone's mother was Demeter, the goddess of crops and harvests. She grieved every year during the time Persephone was in the underworld, and for the Greeks that explained why there were three months of winter each year, with few plants growing.

HERA

Hera was the wife of Zeus, so in the myths she is the queen of the gods. She was the patron of marriage and the household, and the protector of women. She ruled heaven and the world of humans before she married Zeus, so she was powerful in herself, not just because she was his wife.

HERA

Her marriage with Zeus was very rocky, because Zeus often had interest in other gods or in human women. Hera spent a lot of time trying to attack Zeus' favorites, or those like Hercules who were his children but not hers.

ATHENA

Athena was the goddess of intelligence, thought, and wisdom. According to the myth, she sprang, fully-grown, from the head of her father, Zeus.

Athena was a fierce warrior, but she did not like battle and killing in the same way Ares, the god of war, did. She fought to defend or restore justice. Zeus even let her use his powerful thunderbolts when she needed them.

ATHENA

APHRODITE

APHRODITE

Aphrodite was the goddess of beauty and love. She was also the goddess of birth, although she had no children herself. She was married to Hephaestus, the blacksmith of the gods, at Zeus' orders, but she was also interested in Ares, the god of war.

APOLLO

Apollo, a son of Zeus, was the god of music and was known to be a powerful fighter with a magical bow and arrows. He was also the god who drove the chariot of the sun through the sky every day.

APOLLO

pollo was the god of both healing and sickness. He was the patron of prophets and seers: people would visit his oracle at Delphi to try to learn from Apollo what would happen in the future.

To learn more about Apollo, read the Baby Professor book, Apollo's Deadly Bow and Arrow.

ARTEMIS

Artemis was Apollo's twin sister. She is known as the goddess of hunting, and of the love of nature. She was an excellent archer and hunter.

She was born first of the twins, and then immediately helped her mother deliver Apollo. This shows how clever and caring she was from the first moments of her life.

ARTEMIS

ARES

ARES

Ares, a child of Zeus and Hera, was the god of war. He was violent and powerful, always ready to bring down trouble on those who opposed him. However, in the stories, Ares is also a coward and a complainer. He was very much in love with Aphrodite, who was already married to another god, Hephaestus, and this is probably part of why he was so angry all the time.

HERMES

Hermes was the messenger of the gods, a son of Zeus and Maia. He thought and moved quickly, and was very tricky. He enjoyed playing tricks on his fellow gods, and then talking his way out of trouble.

HERMES

HEPHAESTUS

HEPHAESTUS

Hephaestus was the god of creating: of blacksmiths, builders, workmen, artists, and sculptors. He was also the god of volcanoes, fire, and those who work with metal of any kind. Hephaestus, in one myth, is the son of Zeus and Hera. In another story, Hera gave birth to him without a father, and rejected him because he was malformed.

Hephaestus made the weapons and armor that the gods used and wore. He was married to Aphrodite on Zeus' orders, but there was no great love between them.

TEMPLE OF
HEPHAESTUS

GREAT GREEK HEROES

Here are some of the heroes who struggle with both gods and mortals in the Greek myths.

ACHILLES

Achilles was the greatest fighter on the Greek side in the Trojan War. His mother had dipped him into the River Styx, on the border of the underworld, so he could not be wounded--except where she had held his heel while she dipped him. That part of the foot is called "The Achilles tendon" in his honor. Paris, a Trojan prince, shot an arrow into Achilles's heel and killed him.

ACHILLES

HERCULES AND ACHELOUS

HERCULES

Hercules was the son of Zeus and of Alcmene, who was a granddaughter of Perseus. Hercules was a great warrior, strong and skilled, but he was often in trouble because Hera, Zeus' wife hated him.

To learn more about Hercules, read the Baby Professor book Who Was Hercules?

JASON

J ason's uncle took Jason's kingdom from him, and promised to give it back only if Jason brought him the Golden Fleece, wool from a magical winged sheep. Jason and his 50 companions, the Argonauts, travelled to get the Fleece. After many adventures, they succeeded with the help of Medea, a sorceress.

JASON WITH THE GOLDEN FLEECE

ODYSSEUS

After helping the Greeks defeat the Trojans, King Odysseus and his people sailed for Ithaca, their home. The trip should have taken a few weeks, but because of adventures with gods and monsters, the journey took ten years. And once he got home, he had to fight to get his kingdom back.

Learn more about Odysseus and his long trip in the Baby Professor book Interesting Facts about Homer's Odyssey.

PERSEUS

Perseus was a great fighter and very quick-thinking. He defeated many enemies, including the Medusa, a gorgon who would turn you to stone if you looked at her. Perseus fought her while looking at her reflection on his shield!

PERSEUS WITH THE HEAD OF MEDUSA

FILE:THESEUS KILLING MINOTAUR

THESEUS

Theseus is famous for defeating the Minotaur, a monster who lived in a maze on the island of Crete. Each year, until Theseus killed him, the Minotaur ate seven young men and seven young women offered to it as a sacrifice. Theseus later became king of Athens.

ATALANTA

Atalanta was a fast runner, a strong wrestler, and a great archer. She was one of the heroes who went with Jason to find the Golden Fleece, and she is a major character in the story of the hunt of the Calydonian Boar.

Atalanta was very beautiful and many men wanted to marry her. She challenged men to race with her, and none could beat her. Finally, she married Hippomenes, even though she beat even him in a race.

ATALANTA AND HIPPOMENES

HERCULES OBTAINING
THE GIRDLE OF HYPPOLITA

HIPPOLYTA

The Greeks believed there was a tribe of warrior women who lived somewhere around the Black Sea, and that Hippolyta was their queen. Hippolyta was a daughter of the god Ares.

When Hercules had to bring back the girdle, or belt, of Hippolyta as one of his Twelve Labors, he did not just bring back the rich, jewelled belt. He captured Hippolyta and brought her back to Greece as well. Eventually Theseus, now king of Athens, married her.

PENTHESILEA

Penthesilea was one of Hippolyta's sisters. In the Trojan war, she led the Amazons to fight on the side of the Trojans against the Greeks. Achilles killed her in battle, although he admired her beauty and fighting skill.

PENTHESELIA

ADVENTURES AWAIT!

Great heroes need great opponents! Read the Baby Professor book Ancient Greece has Monsters, Too! to learn what these heroes had to face and defeat.

Visit
BABY PROFESSOR
EDUCATION KIDS
www.BabyProfessorBooks.com
to download Free Baby Professor eBooks
and view our catalog of new and exciting
Children's Books